CIVIC CONSERVATISM
David Willetts MP

The Social Market Foundation
1994

First published in June 1994
by
The Social Market Foundation
20, Queen Anne's Gate
London SW1H 9AA
Tel: 071-222 7060 Fax: 071-222 0310

Paper No. 20

ISBN 1 874097 40 2

Cover design by Adrian Taylor

Printed in Great Britain by
Xenogamy plc
Suite 2, Westcombe House
7-9 Stafford Road, Wallington, Surrey SM6 9AN
Typesetting by Wimyk Enterprises

CONTENTS

THE AUTHOR

DAVID WILLETTS is the Member of Parliament for Havant and is Parliamentary Private Secretary to Sir Norman Fowler MP, the Chairman of the Conservative Party.

From 1978 to 1984 he was an official at HM Treasury, from 1984 to 1986 a member of the Prime Minister's No. 10 Policy Unit, and from 1987 to 1992 the Director of Studies at the Centre for Policy Studies.

He has written widely on economic and social policy. His book *Modern Conservatism* was published as a Penguin paperback in 1992.

ACKNOWLEDGEMENTS

The author is very grateful for the advice and encouragement of Daniel Finkelstein and Roderick Nye from the Social Market Foundation in the preparation of this Paper.

Foreword

The counter-revolution against a rationalist, abstract and universalist free market triumphalism continues to gather pace. Evidence of its importance can be seen in the writings of Selbourne on duty; in the thoughts of John Gray on Russia; in the leader columns of *The Times*; in the speeches on the family and civic institutions by politicians across the political spectrum.

Gradually the argument is taking hold that a market economy is defined by the institutions of which it consists and that these institutions are the product of culture, history, law and the conscious activity of statesmen. They also rely upon social consent in its widest sense, as Robert Skidelsky argued in the very first Social Market Foundation paper.

The terms of debate have therefore moved from a narrow and mechanical application of theory to a much richer discussion of the nature of institutions and community. David Willetts shows brilliantly, in Chapter Six of this Paper, how consideration of issues such as behaviour and mutuality fundamentally alters the debate on the welfare state, and posits an alternative to the cutters, spenders and technocrats.

Two connected issues lie at the heart of this new debate. The first is the degree to which free market institutions can survive the rapid adaptation of a global market economy. Does the market sweep away the traditional civic institutions that underpin it? The second concerns the role of politics in sustaining market economies. What values should animate social policy and what instruments should be used to strengthen communal ties and civic responsibility?

David Willetts' paper is published as one of a pair. Dr John Gray argues in his contribution, *The Undoing of Conservatism*, that market liberalism has fatally undermined the stable civic society which alone makes it possible. But in *Civic Conservatism* these arguments are rejected in favour of a more optimistic belief that limited government and free institutions are essential and perfectly consistent partners of free markets.

David Willetts writes from the standpoint of a Conservative MP. This has the advantage of allowing him to draw on traditions of conservative thought which have much to offer any proper consideration of civic institutions. Its disadvantage is that it may discourage others from paying closer attention to his clear and well-expressed vision. This would be a pity. The paper is published by the Social Market Foundation, together with its counterpart, as a contribution from one highly-regarded political thinker to a political debate that is engaging many of very different views. It is also published in the hope, indeed in the confidence, that it will be seen as an important and distinguished piece of work in its own right.

Daniel Finkelstein
June 1994

Chapter One: The Problem Stated

The roots of the difficulties encountered by this Government are not to be found in the last recession, nor indiscipline by the Parliamentary Party, nor any mistakes made by the Government itself. The problem is much deeper and it is ultimately an intellectual one. It is a dangerous uncertainty about the nature of modern Conservatism.

Sometimes this thought is expressed by the observation that we have slain so many dragons — trade union barons, nationalised industries, the Soviet Empire — that we are left without a purpose, victims of our own success. It is as if we have worked ourselves out of a job. But there are still enormous political challenges to face — from strengthening the supply-side of the economy, through addressing the problems of crime and incivility, to raising education standards. To that list could be added those battles which are never over and test the mettle of any government, such as containing the costs of the welfare state and cutting public expenditure. The free market remains relevant to all these issues, but we are not so confident about this as we were.

The real problem is that Conservatives have become wary of relying as heavily on the free market as we appeared to do in the 1980s. It was Marx who first observed that in modern capitalism all relationships became 'commodified'; they all became market transactions. There are many good Conservatives who must now be regarded as sharing this Marxist critique. Their feeling is not that the Government is doing too little, but that it is doing too much. They fear that nothing is to be safe from this market reductionism, be it in the form of market testing, the internal market or ever more ambitious privatisations. Contract culture appears to have triumphed and the accountants rule: that leaves many traditional Conservatives uneasy.

Looking back on the passionate disputes which have dominated the Conservative Party over the past year, two crucial issues stand out. The first of course is Europe and the future of the nation state, which is under pressure as much from the global economy and the logic of the single market as the designs of the federalists. The other issue which lies behind 'back-to-basics', concern about incivility and declining standards of behaviour, single parents and juvenile crime is the future of the family. The family is under pressure from changes in the labour market and ever greater mobility as well as from the explicit anti-family agenda of some. There is a connection between these two issues: the nation-state and the family are the two most significant non-market institutions. They have aroused such passion and confusion because Conservatives believe they cannot be reduced to the imperatives of the market-place: hence the vigour with which Conservatives have leapt to their defence even whilst the 'realists' wonder if the battle can be won and the cynics observe that the real enemy is the free market which the Conservatives have unleashed. No wonder these arguments leave Conservatives feeling a mixture of defiance, alarm and self-doubt. It is the purpose of this paper to show how these uncertainties might be dispelled. That involves keeping the free market at the heart of Conservatism whilst showing how it is compatible with strengthening those institutions and values which can never be reduced to market transactions.

Whenever Conservatives try to draw attention to a social issue, to talk about our shared values and traditions, indeed, whenever we try to talk about anything in politics which goes beyond what would be found in a company's annual report, the critics gleefully pounce: 'you cannot appeal to any sense of community, you cannot talk about values because the biggest threat to these values comes from the free markets which you have unleashed'. As free marketeers, it seems Conservatives are condemned only to talk about profit and loss, not right and wrong. Conservatives need to tackle head on this crucial challenge that markets undermine values, that commerce destroys culture. It is a challenge which touches a particular chord with British Conservatives precisely because the Conservative Party is so long-lived, so intertwined with Britain's history, our country's traditions and institutions. Turning round and accusing us of destroying them by unleashing free markets is painfully perverse.

The argument is often presented as a striking new criticism of the way in which the Conservative Party has developed in the last 20 years but really it has been a theme in British political debate for at least two centuries. Thomas Carlisle denounced what he called 'the Gospel of Mammon' 150 years ago:

> We call it a Society; and go about professing openly the totalest separation, isolation. Our life is not a mutual helpfulness; but rather, cloaked under due laws-of-war, named 'fair competition'

and so forth, it is a mutual hostility. We have profoundly forgotten everywhere that *Cash-payment* is not the sole relation of human beings.

The argument is not merely that free markets are unpleasant: but also that they are pernicious. They are supposed to spread a way of thinking, the market way of thinking, which destroys other values including, ironically, values which capitalism itself needs to thrive. Joseph Schumpeter writing 50 years ago is perhaps the most distinguished exponent of this view:

> Capitalism creates a critical frame of mind which, after having destroyed the moral authority of so many other institutions, in the end turns against its own; the bourgeois finds to his amazement that the rationalist attack does not stop at the credentials of kings and popes, but goes on to attack private property and the whole scheme of bourgeois values. The bourgeois fortress thus becomes politically defenceless.

This is what he believed to be the real internal contradiction of capitalism: it would collapse not, as Marxists wrongly predicted, because the workers became even poorer, but paradoxically because of its own success. It would destroy the very values — deferred gratification, self discipline, respect for promises and contracts — necessary to sustain it. Today's leader writers who attribute all our social ills to the evil effects of a philosophy which they say is just 'Me and Here and Now' are thus placing themselves in a long tradition of denunciations of the market.

Some Conservatives are inclined to reply by playing down the role of the market in Conservative thought, but this is bad history. Edmund Burke went into politics as a follower of Adam Smith and free markets have been at the centre of Conservatism ever since. Nevertheless there is more to Conservatism than the free market.

Conservatism is at its finest and its most distinctive precisely when it integrates a commitment to the free market into the core values and institutions which hold our country together. How we might achieve such a reconciliation is the theme of the rest of this paper.

Chapter Two: Understanding Our History

To understand the role of markets in Conservatism, we also have to understand their role in Britain's history. There are still people who believe the caricature that free markets were discovered by Milton Friedman and then imported to Britain by Keith Joseph and Mrs Thatcher in the late 1970s, like some nasty foreign predator recklessly let loose in our country and destroying our indigenous species. This failure to understand our own history helps explain the tendency for political debate to be distorted by misplaced fears of the damage which the free market might do our traditional institutions.

The historical truth is not just that Britain is a free market society but that it was the first market society. Alan Macfarlane's classic study, *The Origins of English Individualism*, offers a fascinating account of England before the Industrial Revolution. He shows that, unlike the Continent, England never experienced the classic medieval social order: there were no English serfs. Free men were selling their labour and exchanging land all through the Middle Ages, and when, at the Stuart Restoration, leasehold under the Crown was converted to freehold, this was the final recognition of a long established reality. (The picture in Scotland and Ireland was rather different — a point that is relevant to other political debates, but which need not detain us now). To believe that Britain underwent the Industrial Revolution and then became a free market economy is to misunderstand the historical process. Britain was the first free market society and was thus ripe for the Industrial Revolution.

One piece of evidence in support of this interpretation, which is directly relevant to today's policy arguments about the environment, is the network of property rights in the countryside. American environmentalists have now recognised that one of their biggest problems is that much of the Mid West belongs to the Federal Government and does not have enlightened owners concerned to maintain the value of their property. They look with envy at the intricate network of property rights established in England by the end of the Middle Ages — fishing rights, hunting rights, laws of trespass, laws about the use of common land. The beauty of the English countryside is a testament to the work of centuries of inherited property rights. By contrast, as Alice Coleman has shown, the desolation and alienation of an inner city estate is a direct consequence of the lack of clear property rights.

When Adam Smith wrote *The Wealth of Nations* he was challenging a contemporary economic doctrine — mercantilism — but his own insights matched Britain's historical experience over previous centuries. That may help explain why his ideas were absorbed so easily by what was to become the Conservative party. Edmund Burke, the High Tory, was also the author of the free market *Notes on Scarcity* and the advocate of what he called 'economical reform' to eliminate waste in the public sector. Adam Smith famously observed of Edmund Burke 'that he was the only man who, without communication, thought on these topics exactly as he did'. Pitt the Younger, Liverpool and Peel pursued a policy of free trade, tax-cutting, deregulation and tight monetary control that would now be called monetarism. This project was part of sweeping away the old patronage style politics of the 18th Century and creating instead a model of limited government. The high moral tone of Victorian politics was not achieved by accident — it was a direct consequence of the success of the free market project in reshaping British institutions in the first half of the 19th Century. The 'Old Corruption' was associated with heavy Government involvement in the economy; free market reforms did not just strengthen the economy but also raised the tone of political debate.

As we wrestle today with the problems of urban incivility, shiftless young men and a sense that powerful economic forces are wrenching apart an established social order, we should remember that the Victorians went through similarly dramatic changes. They experienced rapid industrialisation, the biggest population movements in our history, the emergence of enormous new cities, together with a population boom that gave Victorian society an age profile as youthful as in the Third World today. They saw themselves as 'shooting the rapids' — and on the far side was a civil and democratic society in which everyone participated: there was to be no permanent urban underclass. They were extraordinarily successful in moralising the urban poor without heavy-handed use of government (which indeed they saw as part of the problem). Drunkenness, crime and illegitimacy all fell during the second half of the nineteenth century — the high point of limited government and free trade.

Some Conservatives reacted to the instability and dynamism of Victorian England by a retreat into nostalgia for a medieval past. Disraeli and the Young England movement of the 1840s hoped for a return to a sort of medieval community as an alternative to industrialism. Nostalgia is a powerful and indeed legitimate political appeal. In a country with a history like ours, where the National Trust is the largest voluntary association, any politician is going to be tempted to mould his arguments in the form of an appeal to the past. We see it in today's debates about social change. If some Conservatives look back to 'real families' of a man earning a family wage and his wife at home looking after their children, so the Labour party looks back nostalgically to 'real jobs', when the man was working all his adult years on the production line of some heavy industry which has long since gone to the Third World. The irony is that those traditional jobs and those traditional families went together and neither can easily be sustained without the other.

Nowadays one might think that for the Labour party the ideal is the 1940s and for the Conservatives it is the 1950s. The critics may attack Conservatives for looking back fondly to those potent images of life in the suburbs of the 1950s; but anyone following the work of left wing intellectuals such as David Hare can see that for them the period to celebrate is what is thought to have been the intense national community of the wartime years and immediately afterwards.

There are still lessons to be learnt from the historical debates of the 1940s and 1950s. Richard Titmuss gave the classic Socialist interpretation of the 1940s, arguing that 'the circumstances of the War created an unprecedented sense of social solidarity among the British people, which made them willing to accept a great increase of egalitarian policies and collective state intervention'. But there are two problems with this claim. First, wartime may create an intense sense of national purpose, but it is no model for the life of a civil society in peacetime. To regard a society at war as any sort of model for peacetime is to take a dangerous step on the path to totalitarianism: the tragedy was that the War confirmed us in our fatal trust in government as benign and rational. Secondly, there was a good deal more detachment, scepticism, cynical humour in the 1940s than is now allowed for. Ministry of Information surveys of popular attitudes at the time show that people were most concerned about their personal and family safety and about winning the war, rather than with issues of social justice or post-war reconstruction.

If we move on to look at the 1950s we can see the national mood was extraordinarily sensitive to fears about the damage done by free markets and remarkably relaxed about the damage done by big government. The pundits feared that commercial television was going to threaten our national culture. Looking back we can see that it was the destruction of the old communities by the enormous new public sector housing estates, a bipartisan policy trusting to big government, which did far more damage. Throughout the post-war period public debate in this country has been preoccupied with the damage to traditional British values supposedly threatened by brash market forces whilst at the same time the real threat was coming from the intrusive state. It is as if, like the guns of Singapore, we are armed against the wrong enemy, ready to repel an assault from the forces of vulgar American capitalism, whilst our society has really been under threat from the enormous powers of our own state.

When the historians finally reach a detached assessment of the 1980s the picture will look very different than the conventional wisdom now. At the moment we are told it was all about the triumph of market forces. The truth about the 1980s is that the serious policy mistakes came from the drift away from free markets. Especially after the 1987 General Election, the Government passed too much bad law — bad laws which shared the common feature of giving ever more power to the state. Government was imposing new costs on the private sector, but instead of showing up as increased public expenditure, the costs were imposed through heavy-handed regulation: they might not appear on the fiscal balance sheet but they were just as real to the private sector. The Financial Services Act, the Children Act, the Charities Act, the Food Safety Act all imposed heavy new burdens on the private sector without any rational calculation of costs and benefits. The idea of the state as enabler, purchaser or contractor, contains a great deal of sense, as we shall see in a later chapter. But it must not be distorted by the pernicious belief that Whitehall knows best and thus become a ground for yet more heavy-handed intrusion in the affairs of civil society.

How did the 1980s compare with the 1970s? In the 1970s the government was spending a higher percentage of GDP and was intervening in the economy far more. Did this somehow enable us to achieve a moral consensus as a nation, a greater sense of community? Was there less materialism and greed? Far from it, instead we had a Hobbesian war of all against all, fought with the state as the battleground. Each interest group was trying to capture the state for its own purposes — obtaining subsidies or tax breaks. As a result we suffered from the twin and related evils of overloaded government and ungovernability. In trying to do too much government merely found itself caught between a multitude of inconsistent claims for 'social justice'. Rolling back the frontiers of the state was essential for restoring some degree of authority to government.

The conclusion to this brief historical excursion is a paradox. On the one hand Great Britain has a longer history and experience of free market transactions than any other society in the world. But equally we seem not to understand our own history and perpetually to fall a prey to the belief that we need our government to intervene to protect us from these dark, hostile, outside forces. As a result we are always on the lookout for the threat from market forces and are remarkably slow to see the greater danger posed for our civil society from the encroachment of the state.

Chapter Three: The Market & Beyond

The previous chapter tried to show that the free market is an integral part of our history. Conservatives who worry about the impact of the free market on our traditions need to recognise that the free market itself is at the heart of the British tradition. But not only does the free market suffer from misconceptions about its place in our history, it also suffers from misconceptions about its claims as economic theory. We need to get straight exactly what free market economics really claims and whether it is compatible with any recognition of values and institutions which stand outside the market.

The first crucial distinction is between the free market as an abstract model and as a real set of institutions and human actors. The free market is one of the most powerful analytical tools which the social sciences have developed; but market transactions only take place within a real set of institutions, a culture, a tradition. Academic economists have by and large been uninterested in the cultural and institutional underpinnings of real markets (shown for example in their extraordinary naiveté about economic reform in the old Soviet bloc). It is free marketeers with an understanding of Conservatism who are best placed to explore these connections between the market as it appears in economic theory and the market as a social reality. This makes it all the more surprising that Conservatives failed during the 1980s to show how we understood these essential underpinnings to the market. It is what distinguishes us from pure economic liberals who see us all simply as individual economic agents floating freely, untrammelled by ties, culture or history. It is the aim of this chapter to explore the links between the abstract model of economic transactions and the reality of the market as an institution. The aim is to show how market transactions may only happen within an institutional framework and that market transactions themselves can help to sustain non-market institutions and values.

Arnold Toynbee offered a vivid and repellent picture of the free market: it is a world inhabited by 'gold-seeking animals, stripped of every human affection, forever digging, weaving, spinning, watching with keen undeceived eyes each others' movements, passing incessantly and easily from place to place in search of gain, all alert, crafty, mobile.' That captures how many of today's critics of the free market see it. We are all supposed to be atomistic individuals, pursuing our own self interest and incapable of recognising any ties to people and institutions which are more than economic. On this sort of model the free market is at best an unpleasant necessity: it would deserve no place at the heart of Conservatism.

This visceral British suspicion of the free market rests on serious misunderstandings of free market economics. For a start, free market economics is not an account of human motivation. It has no pretensions to be a psychological theory. Believers in free markets are no more committed to saying that everyone is motivated by personal greed than to saying that every tennis player at Wimbledon is simply motivated to win by the prize money. The players may be driven by any emotion from pride to wishing to please their parents, but we can say that, by and large, the best tennis comes from matches in which the players compete to win within the framework of the rules.

Free market thinkers have gone beyond this, however, and shown how even without appealing to such attractive qualities as benevolence or altruism and simply using the highly schematic model of us as economic agents, it is still possible to offer an account of the emergence of co-operative institutions. This is because within a competitive environment, co-operative behaviour may be the most efficient. Institutions which have a non-market logic of their own may thrive within a market environment.

Let us go back to the tennis match, but this time it is a game of doubles. One couple are radical individualists, each of them goes for every shot, they shamelessly poach off each other and each of them is concerned much more about how he or she performs than about their performance as a unit. On the other side of the net is a much more co-operative couple, they respect their partner, give way to each other, understand that each of them is only one part of a greater unit — the team. The chances are that a ruthlessly competitive tennis match will reveal the weaknesses of the first couple and recognise the competitive strength of the co-operative couple.

This is clearly relevant to the experience of modern capitalism. A Western businessman was describing to the author how his factory had been visited by a delegation of industrialists from the old Soviet bloc. What had amazed them above all was that the workers on the shop floor were not directly and continuously supervised. In the East the only way to ensure that a factory worker worked hard was to have a foreman almost literally standing over him — a sort of industrial equivalent of the secret police. This was not only unpleasant, it was also an incredibly wasteful way of running an enterprise. It makes much more sense if employees are motivated, feel part of a larger team to which they are committed, and want to do their best.

Modern management techniques are precisely about creating a sense of co-operation and teamwork within the enterprise, because it is those types of enterprises which enjoy enormous efficiency gains and are thus rewarded in the open competitive market place. This is where the case of Japan fits in. We are often told that Japan is a model of capitalism very different from that in the West: let us assume, for the sake of argument, that that is true. We are told that we need to learn from Japan that lifetime employment, a commitment to the long term, not to mention worship of the company god, are all much better than traditional Anglo-Saxon capitalism. But what is the evidence that it is better? The evidence is that Japan has been an enormous economic success. Many of its industries have outperformed our own. Japan's institutional arrangements are rewarded in a competitive market environment. Now many firms in the West are trying to learn from Japanese industrial practices and absorb them. This shows that modern capitalism does not necessarily destroy ties of affiliation and loyalty but may well reward them because they also happen to be efficient.

The market makes no moral judgement about these arrangements, even though we personally will want to. But it does force us to focus on one of the big issues in economic and political theory — the point at which external, market-based contractual arrangements should cease and internalised arrangements based on co-operation or authority should take over. Modern economic theory of the firm focuses above all on defining the boundaries which determine where external market style transactions should be displaced by internalised transactions based on authority, co-operation or teamwork. The firm constitutes one boundary where the market stops. The firm is, in the language of economists, itself a sort of 'market failure'.

This choice between an internal model of co-operation and an externalised market model is not a choice between good and evil, altruism and selfishness. The market itself is, in a sense, a co-operative institution in that it enables people with diverse, backgrounds, purposes and desires to serve each others' interests through free exchange. For the wheels of capitalism — specialisation of labour and trade — to turn, it is necessary that economic agents have different skills and tastes. It is the paradox of co-operation through the free market that it is co-operation with people we may not know and whose tastes and values may be very different from our own — the people who have made my child's toy may be living on the other side of the world in a culture far removed from my own.

Capitalism integrates us into what is rapidly becoming a single global economy. It creates a sort of community of interest without creating a community of values or of sympathy. For the pessimist it will be depressing that it does not necessarily create a community of values amongst market participants. But for the optimist the achievement will be that even when no shared values are to be found, there is nevertheless the possibility, through market transactions, of working together for mutual benefit.

The boundaries between this internal and externalised co-operation are permanently shifting in response to a range of cultural and technological influences. The biggest single influence is probably the best way of handling information. Modern technology has made explicit pricing possible in areas where that was not possible before. Within a decade we will probably be paying directly for tap-water by the gallon, for each individual television programme that we watch, and for every half mile that we drive on a crowded city road. That is not some evil aggrandisement by the market; it is just that the costs of collecting the information necessary to price these goods and services is falling so dramatically that it will be possible to bring them fully within the range of the market. But equally in some other areas of human life, the advance of technology has caused a retreat from market transactions. We now use equipment within our own homes to cook or clean for ourselves what many households would have paid servants for a century ago. The cost of a washing machine is now so low relative to the cost of a washer-woman that by and large the labour market has withdrawn from these transactions. In Chapter Seven of this paper I shall explain how these arguments are relevant to the internal organisation and structure of the public sector.

So far, we have clarified three particular features of the market. First, it is not a theory of human motivation: market participants can have an enormous variety of purposes. Secondly, the market can itself reward co-operative behaviour as it may also be efficient. Thirdly, the boundaries which divide internal institutional arrangements for ensuring that people serve each others' purposes and external market-style arrangements will permanently be shifting. It is wrong to regard such shifts as somehow a battle between good and evil.

There is a fourth point to add to this list, and this is that the market will also create circumstances which favour co-operation in another way — by the very process of mobility itself. Mobility is perhaps the most significant aspect of a market of all and it is the most ambiguous in its effects. Let us start with the obvious appeal of mobility, which nobody now can resist — that it enables the individual to make his or her own way in the world, seizing the benefits of equality of opportunity which no one nowadays could possibly oppose. The market hates waste and the greatest waste of all is people who are not given the opportunity of realising their potential. The most powerful force for breaking down the barriers of discrimination by sex or race or background is the market itself which will not want talents to go to waste. These are the roots of a modern, mobile and meritocratic society.

The irony is however that it is precisely this liberating power of the market, so widely welcomed, which also helps to explain some of our worse discontents. Consider how the concept of the 'ghetto' has changed over the past fifty years. A traditional ghetto was an entire group suffering systematic discrimination, such as Jews in Europe, or black people in America. It developed its own sense of community, its own hierarchies and sense of order as everyone, regardless of their abilities, found themselves trapped in the same way. What happens to such a ghetto if the barriers start to come down and suddenly its inhabitants can move in every sense — geographically, economically, and socially? The people with drive, exceptional ability, self-confidence take their chance and move out. What is left behind is a ghetto transformed into something far worse than existed before — the people who are finding it hard to command a good income in an increasingly meritocratic society and who find themselves without community leaders and models of success to look up to and hold their community together. They lose out as the institutions which would give a shape to their communities and their lives are weakened. That is why the Harlem of the 1990s is a much worse place than the Harlem of the 1940s. And on a much less dramatic scale such forces have been at work in our country as well. The clearest case is probably the Catholics of Northern Ireland where, as the barriers have come down, we at last see a successful, well-integrated Catholic middle class. The Catholic communities left behind suffer the same sort of social collapse in some of the black inner cities of America.

The problems of social collapse in inner city areas and sink estates have been widespread across advanced Western economies since the War. It is a testament to the shallowness of the British preoccupation with public spending and the state that so many people here analyse these problems solely in terms of public spending, social security benefits and public sector house building. The truth is that we can only understand these problems if we appreciate that they are linked to the mobility and openness which is one of the most attractive features of a modern free market economy.

It would be wrong to stop the analysis there, because it is misleading to focus on the effects of moving away from communities without also looking at the strength of communities which people move to. Most people have seized the chance to live in the sort of communities they want to live in, with the sort of neighbours they want to have. This brings people together in new communities of choice rather than of circumstance. It is a change from which many people in our country have derived great benefit.

The market order which we have been describing may not always be moral, or beautiful — though it is usually elegant and efficient. But neither is it pernicious or evil. It is non-moral rather than immoral. It is the background against which individuals and institutions must pursue their purposes. The Church, wrestling with the problem of the cost of maintaining surplus churches in areas where the church-going population is shrinking, or the academic wondering at what price to sell his book attacking Thatcherism are confronting the laws of supply and demand in the same way as the businessman selling his widgets. If we accept it as the essential environment within which we all must pursue our purposes, then political debate will finally have escaped from tedious and sterile opposition to the market.

Chapter Four: Civic Conservatism

The free market is the cutting edge of modern Conservatism. It is the free market above all which has yielded much of the intellectual creativity and political dynamism of Conservatism over the past two decades. But many of the uncertainties and confusions in Conservatism at the moment come from a creeping recognition that the free market, like patriotism, is not enough.

Values ranging from particular virtues, like honesty and fairness, through to ties of affinity to the wider community, constrain the market. These values are sustained by non-market institutions which help to shape our behaviour. And the free market actually needs these values in order to operate: they provide the cultural and moral environment it needs. If that environment does not exist then the market itself cannot take root — a problem which is becoming obvious in the old Soviet bloc. If private enterprise has been criminal for 75 years it is very difficult to create a new understanding of the boundaries between commerce and crime. If money lacks any sense of legitimacy, commerce just seems a refined form of theft — and that is a poor base on which to build a modern free market economy.

The pernicious error, upheld by so many of our *bien pensants* and pundits, is to regard the market as the threat to the rich life of a civil society and the state as somehow embodying or protecting those values. The historical evidence offered in Chapter Two and the economic theory explained in Chapter Three show what a fallacy this is. The tragedy of 20th Century Britain has been the way in which the state has taken over and then drained the life blood from a series of institutions which stood between the individual and the government. In his fascinating book on the British Constitution, Ferdinand Mount subtly analyses what he calls the 'thinning' of our understanding of the British Constitution. Instead of appreciating all the checks and balances of a civil society we have moved over the past century simply to a belief in the over-arching power of a Sovereign Parliament. But that process has not just gone on in our constitutional theory: we have seen it in practice too as our network of civic institutions has also thinned. Gradually we have lost sight of the virtues of those institutions which thicken our social structure and give it a richness which is lost if it is just individuals facing a Fabian, centralised welfare state. Britain has been, if you like, 'deconstructed'. We have seen great and proud institutions such as our voluntary hospitals nationalised and brought under state direction: it is no exaggeration to say that Bart's fate was sealed when it was nationalised in 1948 and lost control of its own destiny, becoming the tool of health planners. Other institutions like our ancient universities have become so dependent on public funds that they have fallen a prey to the disease of believing that the best way to embarrass politicians into giving more money is to say how terrible things are. The behaviour of too many public sector bodies and their associated pressure groups reminds one of those nature programmes showing fledglings in a nest with beaks permanently open to attract the harassed parent. And as resources are inevitably finite, the battle is really to attract attention away from their rival siblings — a stark truth which is ignored in polite society. Once an institution has descended to this level, it has indeed come to resemble a dependent infant and should not be surprised if it loses authority and respect.

The starting point for any authentically Conservative approach has to be that Britain is not a lumpy enough country. The rationalist agenda for the public sector throughout most of this century has been to eliminate diversity which was always seen as indefensible discrepancy. Reformers have seen themselves as energetic pastry cooks, wielding a rolling pin to smooth out the lumps in the dough. They have ended up producing a state which is smoother, more fine-ground, than any other in the advanced Western world. England does look like a remarkably uniform unitary state compared with other advanced Western countries. In America there is a genuinely federal system. On the Continent the effects of large public sectors are softened by a much greater degree of local discretion than we have here. Germany has different rates of payment for health insurance in different sickness funds. In France a significant element of the welfare system is under the control of the local commune, where the mayor has enormous discretion. In Italy the local tax base is much sturdier than the national tax system. England seems to be neither one thing nor the other; it is too big for central government to have any genuine knowledge of local conditions, but not big enough, not spaced out enough for genuine local diversity to come easily.

This process has not just undermined old institutions like Bart's and ancient universities. As we industrialised in the nineteenth century, a network of voluntary organisations was created by working class self-help: friendly societies, mechanics institutes, local guilds. Macaulay summarised it very well:

This is the age of societies. There is scarcely one Englishman in ten who has not belonged to some association for distributing books, or for prosecuting them; for sending invalids to the hospital, or beggars to the treadmill; for giving plate to the rich, or blankets to the poor.

They have all been weakened, if not destroyed by the advance of the state. And the tragedy is even more poignant because people still do not understand what has happened. Dr David Green (who has studied this subject in great depth) cites a radio programme in which it was argued that it was a disgrace to a civilised society that the Royal National Institute for the Blind was providing services for blind people which should be done by the state. But the real sign of a civilised society is precisely that voluntary, charitable organisations can meet human needs without coercive taxation and the employment of public officials. The way in which public debate about any social problem focuses almost entirely on levels of public spending is depressing evidence of how public understanding of these issues has also 'thinned'. It is a shift in understanding which Conservatives need to combat.

There is a paradox also about these civil institutions which may help to explain why they have lost out in public debate this century. We value qualities — honesty, prudence, generosity — which stretch out way beyond our particular neighbourhood. Moreover we take pride in our identity as citizens of a nation state. And so the government seems to occupy a superior position in the scheme of things because it can support or enforce patterns of behaviour which are uniform and nation-wide. But the truth is that it may be local institutions exercising power and authority locally which are better able to sustain those values than nation-wide institutions. A detailed and over-prescriptive national curriculum might be a less effective device for raising standards in education nation-wide than giving local head teachers greater power in the running of their own schools, and parents the greatest possible power to choose between them.

The challenge facing both our main political parties now is to formulate a coherent set of policies which shows that, as well as for the individual, there must be a role for collective action, but that collective action does not necessarily mean state action. The race is on. And as it is being run, the first thing to remeber is that those institutions which stand between the individual and the state, giving life so much of its meaning, thrive in a free economy where they are not weakened by the burden of high taxes and the suffocating bear hug of high spending. The biggest threat to collective action comes from the state.

Civic Conservatism thus places the free market in the context of institutions and values which make up civil society. Conservatives believe in the free market but as a part of a civil society with limited government and free institutions. One name for this line of thought which may spring to mind is the social market, especially as this paper is published by the Social Market Foundation. The Ordo-Liberal exiles from Hitler's Germany who coined the term understood, as their name implies, that a market has to function as part of the social order. It can only function, for example, if prices carry out their essential job of conveying micro-economic information, hence the crucial role of the independent central bank. Equally, strong and stable families are part of this social order, hence the ambitious Family Law in Germany explicitly setting out obligations between the generations in a family.

Nevertheless there are two difficulties with the term 'social market'. The first is the fatal ambiguity as to whether 'social' is being used as a qualifier or a describer. The Ordo-Liberals meant by the social market a genuinely free market which would thus, by definition, be able to fulfil its social purpose, rather than Hitler's corporatism serving the interests of the military-industrial complex. But in this country the 'social' in 'social market' is taken to carry a rather different implication — that somehow the market is a bitter pill which has to be sweetened with large dollops of public expenditure and state intervention. This misunderstanding of the 'social' is evidence of the impoverished state of our political language.

The second difficulty with the concept of the 'social market' is that it is difficult to detach it from its German origins. The reconstruction of Germany after the War has been one of the triumphs of Western political design, only rivalled by the construction of the United States of America after their War of Independence. In both cases a new political order needed new political and philosophical foundations. The 'social market' was a concept which carried out this role for the Germans. But in Britain, because of the extraordinary continuity of our political and legal arrangements the bonds which tie us together are much more historical and less conceptual. One of the problems which our rationalist reformers encounter is that they imagine that somehow we could all unite behind some explicit new constitutional settlement, without having undergone the crisis of military defeat or rebellion from our sovereign power.

Oddly enough at the same time as the Germans were developing the idea of the social market economy the One Nation Group was formulating a set of ideas which constitute one of the high points of Conservatism. The role of the One Nation Group has been widely misunderstood in the Conservative party. It was not a bunch of what would now be called 'Wets', but instead a group of young Conservative thinkers, such as Enoch Powell, Angus Maude and Iain Macleod, who were rebelling against Baldwinian corporatism, and the nearly Bennite socialism of Harold Macmillan's tract, misleadingly called *The Middle Way*. They stated in 1950:

> To a Tory the nation is not primarily an economic entity. It may place political and social ends above purely economic ones, and for their sake may justifiably on occasions seek to prevent change or divert it. Yet economic change is the normal environment in which nations live, and successful adjustment to it is a condition of their well being. In six years of war and six of socialism this important truth was dangerously obscured and overlaid. We doubt if it yet claims sufficient attention.

This Conservative insight, a commitment to the free market, sustained by a wider set of values and in turn enabling institutions to thrive free of state control is at the heart of Conservatism. It stands in clear contrast to two other positions — Neo-Liberalism and traditionalist Communitarianism.

Conservatives have made a useful alliance of convenience with the free market Neo-Liberals and fought many of the battles of the 1980s with them. But a Conservative realises that, in Quintin Hogg's neat expression economic Liberalism is 'very nearly true'. The trouble with the Neo-Liberals is that they simply think in terms of the individual economic agent without any understanding of the institutions, values and ties which are not just good in themselves but are anyway essential for any real free market to thrive. They suffer from what T H Green called 'inveterate irreverence'. Everything is equally open to challenge. No distinction is made between the trade union closed shop and the Royal Family, between the dangers of welfare dependency and the entitlement to the contributory pension. The real debate within the Conservative Party is precisely about reaching these discriminating judgements and identifying where we need market reform and where not. In doing so we are addressing what Disraeli in *Coningsby* called the 'awkward question' of 'what will you conserve?'

One of the most significant intellectual events of the past five years, which has passed largely unnoticed is the collapse of Neo-Liberalism as a significant intellectual force within this country. Its fountainhead, the Institute of Economic Affairs, is now producing works by ethical Socialists in praise of the family and by anguished Catholic capitalists. It was extraordinary how last year's Conservative party conference was described as moving to the Right, when the real significance of the party conference was that it showed that leading figures on the Right of the party were recognising that there was more to Conservatism than the free market — they were keen to talk about the values which helped sustain a free market economy.

The other alternative now experiencing something of a revival is a rampant Communitarianism which is perpetually on its guard against the market, which it treats as a threat to everything Conservatives hold dear. Its most distinguished and attractive exponent is Dr John Gray. If the peril of the neo-Liberals is their undiscriminating scepticism, the equal and opposite peril of these Communitarians is to 'utopianise the present'. Anything which exists now, provided it has a history of more than about five minutes, is praised in a sub-Oakeshottian prose and absorbed into the precious web of British national identity. Any attempt to change it is to be denounced as cultural vandalism. This view fails to appreciate the cohesive and dynamic role of the market and instead tries to protect us from what it sees as the market's barbarity and harshness. The trouble is that it can lead to the dangerous temptation to opt out from the market environment within which individuals and indeed whole nations must inevitably make their way. Because by and large in British history our governments have been benign, not dragging us into evil wars, or in the words of Queen Elizabeth I 'making windows into men's souls', the communitarian underestimates just how much damage big government can do. We are all aware now of the damage which modern industrial power can do to the environment; but perhaps we do not yet have a sufficient sensitivity to the damage which enormous concentrations of economic, political and legislative power in the hands of government can do to our moral and cultural environment. Even when we try to do good we may do harm. As has been observed, in the past we used to suffer from social evils, now we suffer from our remedies for them.

The Conservatism of all the great British Conservative thinkers, from David Hume and Adam Smith through to Enoch Powell and Michael Oakeshott is an attempt to avoid the twin perils of crude neo Liberalism and a retreat into the cosy embrace of big government as the only vehicle to protect our cultural identities. That commitment both to the free market and to some wider sense of community provides the creative tension which means that this Conservatism, Civic Conservatism, yields more practical insights than either of its simpler alternatives. It is by its practical relevance that Civic Conservatism is best judged and it is to that which I now turn.

The theme of this investigation of Civic Conservatism is the right institutional environment which a free market needs in order to thrive and which in turn can only thrive under a free market. The practical applications of such an approach are particularly relevant to three current political topics — the conduct of economic policy, the future of Europe, and our own anxieties about social change here.

The transformation in the Treasury's approach to economic policy-making over the past 10 years has been dramatic. In the 1980s, when the author served as an official in HM Treasury, the Treasury saw itself as holding a monopoly of economic policy-making. Because of the Treasury's responsibility for public expenditure control, it had become used to regarding every outside body as just a pressure group talking its own book and after either public money or legislative favours. Macro-economic policy-making was a matter of formulating the right financial rules and then sticking to them. The Treasury view has shifted very dramatically over the past few years. It is now understood that one of the best ways of assessing whether or not the economy is in an unsustainable boom, or whether it has the prospects for continuing low inflationary growth, is to judge the amount of spare capacity in the economy, the gap between what the economy could produce and what it is actually producing. That in turn requires close contact with industry and taking their views seriously. Setting aside the Government's wider interest in improving our competitiveness, a dialogue with industry therefore helps the Treasury's ability to deliver the right financial policy.

In addition, the focus for the conduct of monetary policy has shifted from rules towards institutions. In the past we thought that you got credibility by publishing a rule and sticking to it. Now we understand that you can get credibility not by setting up the Treasury as the sole arbiter of financial policy but by bringing a greater interplay of different opinions and institutions into the formulation of policy. That is the reasoning behind creating a panel of independent forecasters and it also lies behind the move towards giving the bank of England a greater degree of practical independence. These changes could be summarised as a shift in economic policy away from achieving credibility through rules towards achieving credibility through institutional diversity.

Similar institutional issues come up in the debate about the future of Europe. Again, some theorists seem to be suffering from serious misapprehensions about what a free market Europe should look like. Some free marketeers, influenced more by the perfect competition of the text books than by the understanding of real competition from economists of the Austrian school, can only think of competition in terms of a level playing field. That is not just a ghastly cliché; it is positively misleading as an account of how a competitive market works. It is not necessary for free competition that employees in competing firms all have the same terms of employment, that their firm have identical legal obligations, let alone that the employees all drink tap water of the same purity. People with that sort of model of genuine competition soon end up concluding that we should ban imports from the Third World as that is 'unfair' competition. In reality, competition is precisely about competition between different ways of doing things, different economic and social arrangements.

The secret of Europe's dynamism over the past few centuries has been precisely that it comprised a series of different nation states — no one authority could suppress scientific experiment or free thought across the whole of Europe. If your prince did not like what you were saying, you could always flee over the border to another country where you could practice your religion or carry out your researches freely. That should equally be the source of Europe's economic vigour. It is not that Britain wants to be the sweatshop of Europe — hourly pay rates are by no means the heart of the economic argument — it is much more to do with the ability to employ labour flexibly and have the legal framework that we want. Again, a diverse Europe with genuine national differences is better than one where all differences have been rolled out by some manic groundsman pursuing that vision of a perfectly level playing field.

There is not space within the confines of this paper to develop these arguments in the areas of economic or European policy. Instead, the rest of the paper will focus on social policy questions and how Civic

Conservatism may contribute in practice to our understanding of these social issues as a given indicator of sensible ways of trying to address them.

Chapter Five: What Kind Of People Are We?

Our deepest fear about the direction our country is taking is that somehow we are becoming worse people — more self-centred, more aggressive, hostile to excellence and achievement, less civil, less willing to give time and effort to any cause greater than ourselves. We see faces in the street or at the wheel of a car with the coarse brutality of a soldier or a peasant in the background of a painting by Breughel.

How real is this change? Are we indeed experiencing what one book has entitled 'a loss of virtue'? If there is a change, is it to be attributed to the free market? What if anything can government do about it? Perhaps no questions are so important, and none more difficult for a politician to address because we have no special claims to moral superiority. But the issues are so important that even politicians must be allowed to comment on them.

The critics normally muddle up two completely inconsistent arguments. First, they claim that terrible changes are indeed happening and the blame lies with the free market — a claim which we have already reviewed. Then if ever a Conservative dare suggest that there is a problem then they are accused of whipping up a 'moral panic' and told that really there is not a problem at all. Yet clearly something is happening and we need to try to be clear what it is.

Three big social changes between them capture people's worries about the character of our lives — family change, long term unemployment and increasing crime. We will look at them briefly in turn and then see how they come together in what some people would call an 'underclass'.

Most of us spend most of our childhood in a household headed by a married couple. Most of us marry and have children. Most people still believe that it is best to get married when you want to have children. It is not that we have opted out from marriage, but rather that extra periods of rather different ways of living have been added to the life cycle. Instead of leaving the family home in order to get married, we leave the family home to live in lodgings or share a flat with other people in our age group. At the other end of the life cycle, as men die before women, there are a large number of widows living on their own, who do not appear in those statistics for households headed by a married couple. These extra stages to the life cycle mean that just a quarter of all households now consist of a married couple with dependent children as against 38% of all households in 1961. The inference we are supposed to draw from this widely-quoted statistic is that we now encounter a rainbow of divergent lifestyles in place of the traditional family. But if we turn from measuring households to measuring people we see that 75% of the British population still live in a household headed by a married couple, a relatively modest decline from 82% in 1961. The biggest changes have been longer transitions in and out of the family — above all a gap between leaving the parental home and establishing a new family home and then, much later, a longer period of widowhood.

More children are being brought up in families which break down or where their father has never been around. Of the 1.3 million lone parents in 1991 the biggest single group, and the one increasing most rapidly, was the unmarried mothers, of whom there were 440,000, approximately a third of the total, as against 170,000 in 1981 and 80,000 in 1971. Nobody, apart from the most constrained prisoner of political correctness, can seriously imagine that being a young, unmarried mother is a good option for either the mother or her child.

The most convincing explanation of the dramatic increase in the number of young, never married, single parents has been offered by the American sociologist, Professor William Julius Wilson. His argument is that the 'marriageable pool' is seriously depleted. Men who are good bets as husbands, ('marriageable' in his terminology), must be holding down a steady job with a good wage. But in the inner cities of America and Great Britain such men are increasingly hard to find. So even if as a woman you want children there is no one it is worth getting married to, to help you bring them up. Another American social thinker, Charles Murray, has added a further element to this explanation. He argues that, at the same time, benefits for single parents and priority access to public housing mean that the option of being a single mother has become easier to sustain. If there are not many reliable men, you can in effect marry the state instead.

One of the reasons for the decline in the pool of marriageable men is of course unemployment. The critics say it is all to do with the recession. One almost wishes the problem was that straightforward: then one could be confident that as the economy grows the problem of young male unemployment would indeed disappear. But even at the height of the boom in the late 1980s we still had pockets of very high rates of male unemployment; and these are the areas where the young lone mothers are concentrated. The reasons for high male unemployment are far removed from the traditional account focusing on the growth rate of the economy. It is much more to do with the problems of young men who themselves may come from unstable family backgrounds, with poor educational achievements and resentment that the only wages they can command are so low. The factors affecting their performance are intangible, not just material. One of the most interesting analyses of the black youth unemployment crisis in inner city America found that the best predictor of whether or not a black youth would find a job, better than social background or educational achievement, was whether he or she went to church. This is an interesting clue, to which we will return later.

The third social problem in our list is crime. We know a surprising amount about criminals. The most obvious fact staring us in the face is that crime is predominantly committed by young men. Professor David Farrington, our leading criminologist, summarises what we know about these juvenile offenders as follows: they tend to be of low intelligence, hyper-active and impulsive; their parents have supervised them poorly with harsh and erratic discipline; their parents are disproportionately likely to be separated and their mother to have given birth as a teenager; they are likely to come from low income families living in over crowded conditions; their parents and siblings are themselves more likely to have a criminal record. A lot of young men will engage in a small amount of crime and a small number of young men will engage in a lot of crime. (The 1% of males born in 1973 who were convicted of six or more offences by the age of 17 accounted for 60% of all convictions for that age group). The peak age of offending is 18 years for men. The peak age of offending actually coincides with a peak of affluence for these young men because they are likely to be in unskilled manual jobs (although their long-term income prospects are not good, their disposable income may well be higher than their peers who are staying on at school or in higher education).

Most young criminals eventually give up crime and settle down. The biggest single reason given for abandoning crime is pressure from a girlfriend or wife. Even after adjusting for all other factors, married men are less likely to be engaged in crime. They also say they stop because penalties are tougher for older, more 'professional' criminals.

Connections are beginning to emerge between these phenomena of changes in the structure of the family, unemployment and crime. Conservatives often become nervous whenever embarking on such observations. The fear which we have — and it is very understandable — is that identifying structural causes risks removing any individual's responsibility for his own actions. But just as a Conservative free marketeer can believe in the laws of supply and demand and at the same time welcome the flair of individual entrepreneurs and businessmen, so we can equally recognise that social and economic forces are at work, even though ultimately every individual's fate remains his or her own responsibility. Conservatives need to develop a much more confident respect for what the lady in the BT advertisement calls 'the ologies' because modern sociology and criminology yield many distinctively Conservative insights.

If we now return to these phenomena of family, unemployment and crime we can see some strong connections. Young men, aged 15 to 25 are the crucial link. They are the ones who are getting the unmarried women pregnant and whom the women — often understandably — have no desire to marry. It is their long term unemployment which causes the greatest instability, particularly in inner city areas, and they are responsible for the vast amount of crime. Whilst there are other social problems, such as the high divorce rate, or the tragedy of unemployed men in middle age or beyond who cannot get back into work, the fact is that the most serious social problems facing us can be traced back to these young males.

Whilst it is tempting to call them an 'underclass' we know that their values are not that different from the rest of us. They are not rebelling against capitalism. They want to settle down, have a good job, bring up a family. They are not highly motivated left wing rebels. (The classic student rebels of the 60s and 70s had, the research now shows, particularly close relationships with their parents whom they respected. Today's young men in trouble are much more likely to come from broken homes and suffer from the absence of an authoritative father figure.) The problem that these young men face is that they cannot get from here to there, they cannot organise their lives or discipline themselves so that they can get from their current circumstances to the sort of life they aspire to. One of their crucial problems is that they lack self-control, they are impulsive. If they see a girl, they grab her, without thinking of the consequences. If they see a hi-fi in a shop they smash the window and grab it. If they are offered a job flipping hamburgers, or delivering pizzas they chuck it in after a short while because they cannot stick at it and do not see why they should accept the low pay.

Some pundits argue that the problem with these young men is that they have become shamelessly individualistic loners. They are the atomised individuals incapable of recognising any ties to anyone other than themselves, who appeared earlier in that vivid quotation from Arnold Toynbee. We have all heard these criminologists and sociologists on the radio and the television saying that all these men are doing is putting into practice Mrs Thatcher's remark that 'there is no such thing as society'. But not only do these people fail to understand the real nature of the free market, they are also factually wrong in their account of how these young men behave. They are sociable and gregarious. This is even apparent in the types of crimes they commit — juvenile crime is group crime. It is the older 'professional' burglar for example who is much more likely to be alone. And one of the reasons they stop offending is that they mature and stop going around in groups. These juvenile delinquents do have loyalties to causes greater than themselves. The trouble is that these deep human instincts to be social, which are as prevalent in a free market society as anywhere else, have been captured almost exclusively by their own peer groups. They hunt and fight in gangs, are influenced by their friends, and will engage in extraordinarily risky behaviour in order to impress them. The trouble is not therefore that they are more self-centred, the problem is that their natural sociability and desire to be regarded by others is not being expressed constructively or creatively.

It is tempting to say that we should be able to prevent this bad behaviour by identifying the trouble-makers at a very early age. We do know that an unstable or broken home increases the risk that someone is likely to get into trouble in their teens and that the earlier someone starts offending the greater the risk. Any infant school teacher worth his or her salt can pick out from their class of six year olds the ones who are likely to be in trouble in ten years time. Indeed one study found that a mother's ratings of her boy's difficult temperament at six months was a good prediction of problems later in childhood. The problem is the false positives. Research shows that teachers will correctly identify the youngsters who are likely to end up as criminals, but they will also identify some who go straight. It is indeed the case that criminals are likely to come from broken homes, but it is a dangerous fallacy to reverse this and say that if you come from a broken home you are likely to be a criminal. It is very difficult to design programmes for groups that are at risk which do not label or assume the worst of children who do have their fates in their own hands and who are not going to make a mess of their lives.

The task facing public policy is therefore clear, albeit enormously difficult to deliver in practice. The challenge is to ensure that these young men make the transition from being children in the parental home to being stable parents themselves without doing too much damage to themselves or the rest of society in the process. That process has become more difficult in modern societies as the transition itself has become more complex with young men spending longer and longer in higher education or training or unemployment before they finally settle down.

The challenge is to create a legal and institutional framework which helps these people come to adulthood. The public sector is failing them if it is largely devoted to helping them systematically avoid ever having to confront the consequences of their actions. It is trapping people in an infantile state in which authority is never exercised, facts are never faced and self-destructive behaviour is tolerated until it is too late. Getting these sort of messages to children by preaching at them is a pretty hopeless task, but it should be possible for them to experience these lessons through their own experience of institutions which are both benign and authoritative. This is where the practical experience of what works in helping young people come to adulthood ties in with the principles of Civic Conservatism set out in previous chapters. It is very difficult for the local institutions which really can help shape people's lives — schools, children's homes, council estates, training schemes, the criminal justice system — to exercise authority if they are systematically being turned into powerless recipients of instructions which come down from a central authority. Let us look at these cases in turn.

Schools are perhaps the most important public institutions of all. All the evidence is that even in the toughest areas a good school can transform people's lives and that in turn the crucial determination of the success of a school is the character of its head teacher. A head teacher needs to be a big figure (which does not necessarily mean authoritarian) who sets standards, inspires the children to live up to them and is aware of that crucial insight of Ernest Bevin's that 'the worst sort of poverty is poverty of aspirations'. Teachers working on the basis that their pupils are going to be systematically discriminated against and will find it very difficult to get jobs will do much less than those who encourage the belief in their children that their future lies in their own hands. It is more difficult now to get away with discipline which is wayward and authoritarian, but a clear framework for behaviour at school, with open rules enforced by all teachers in the same way can make an enormous difference — so-called affirmative discipline programmes have a lot to offer here.

Parents have a remarkable ability to sniff out a good school from a bad school. Unleashing parental choice is the most powerful vehicle of all for improving the quality of schools. Instead of looking up to educational authorities and the Department for Education to tell them what to do, schools instead look out to parents and pupils and work out how they can best satisfy them. A fascinating case study of the power of this approach is Seymour Fleigel's book *Miracle in East Harlem* which describes how a radical liberalisation of the public school system in East Harlem succeeded in raising standards dramatically.

One of the most dramatic ways in which the state has expanded since 1979 is in higher education and training. Training is often recited as a sort of mantra which must inevitably do good, whereas it can do damage in two ways. First, it is no good a central authority deciding what training they think people need if it is not what employers themselves want. Training needs to be driven by individuals choosing what skills they want in order to improve the wage they can command. There is no point creating a system in which people being trained regard themselves as passive and empty vessels being filled whatever way the authorities think best. Secondly, there is some depressing evidence from America which suggests that training programmes for unemployed people can make things worse. In one classic American experiment one group of unemployed people were offered free training whilst the second group were not. A year later it was the unemployed group which had not been offered training who had experienced more success in finding jobs. What is the explanation for this? It appears to be that training programmes do not just increase what the economists call the human capital of trainees, but they also increase their reserve wage, the sort of wage which they feel they ought to command after completing the training course. If the training course is oversold and ends up increasing the reserve wage by more than it increases their real earning capacity then it has created a yet greater obstacle in the way of their finding jobs.

Training schemes can help people in work boost their skills and hence their pay, but they are not always so effective at helping unemployed people find jobs. Indeed, the most effective programme of helping unemployed people back into work is not elaborate training schemes at all, but Job Clubs. They appear to be particularly successful in giving unemployed people that sense of purpose and control of their own lives which helps them into work. They are in many ways the secular equivalent of the evangelical churches whose effect on black unemployment was referred to earlier.

The criminal justice system too often operates like a classic bad parent — unpredictable, wayward, by turns lenient and harsh. Everything we know about juvenile delinquents points to their being classic short termists with no sense of the long-term consequences of their actions. That means they need to experience a criminal justice system which responds rapidly, firmly and predictably to their misbehaviour. Instead too many so-called reforms have made the system ever more long drawn out and incomprehensible. The process between being caught throwing the brick through the window or mugging the old lady and the final punishment is long, complicated and unpredictable. The police have to decide whether or not to let you off with a caution; the probation service has to investigate; the social workers have their say; the court hearing is delayed. By the time the young tearaway ends up in court it seems totally unconnected with the crime he may have committed six months earlier. And then the court hearing itself, which should be charged with significance, can easily degenerate into tedious triviality. Seeing a teenage tearaway appear in court for the first time chastened and worried and then leave a quarter of an hour later with a cheeky smile of relief, as he discovers it does not mean anything after all, gives a depressing sense that one of our last chances of rescuing him has been lost. Much of the debate within the Conservative party about crime focuses on short sharp punishment (useful though that may be) and insufficiently on the need for short, sharp handling of offenders, so that they rapidly confront the consequences of their actions.

In children's homes, the Children Act of 1989 has created doubt among many social workers as to exactly what powers they have physically to restrain children and to exercise authority over them. One police officer assessed the situation very shrewdly. He observed that there was no point ever using excessive force but equally young tearaways in contact with authority had to know that ultimately the people in authority would win. If they knew that beyond a certain point social workers would be powerless to restrain them and had no powers to confine them to the children's home, then they reached the dangerous conclusion that authority could safely be ignored if not mocked.

The theme which connects these particular cases is always that the public sector in its contacts with young people needs to be able to exercise authority and guidance. That is not a matter of being wayward or dictatorial, but it is a matter of the steady exertion of authority and the setting of a clear framework within which young men must live their lives. The local institutions with which young people are in contact need to be authoritative and powerful. But they cannot be like this if they are merely the outposts of an elaborate public sector bureaucracy. Setting them free from centralised control so that they are important local civic institutions is crucial to enable them to do the job of helping shape the lives of the young people with whom they are in contact.

Chapter Six: Welfare & Behaviour

Three different schools of thought dominate the current British debate on the welfare state — the spenders, the cutters and the technocrats.

The spenders believe that the welfare state has enormous power to do good and if more money is spent more good can be done. But they will never accept that it can do any harm. If a social problem is identified, and it is feared welfare spending is making it worse, the welfare state suddenly becomes a puny and irrelevant thing which reacts to people's behaviour but apparently never changes us: it reflects society without affecting it.

Then there are the cutters, who are not interested in the finer points of what the welfare state may or may not be capable. They talk about it as if it is like champagne: it might be marvellous, but the trouble is we simply cannot afford it. In Britain much of the debate about social policies focuses on the cost of the welfare state and relatively little on its social consequences. We are more comfortable talking about the impact of the welfare state on the public finances than on private behaviour.

The third school are the technocrats who have ingenious wheezes — a negative income tax, a social dividend, a new hypothecated tax — all of which seem to solve the taxing and spending dilemma by muddling them up so it is impossible to tell what is being paid in and what is being paid out. These elaborate schemes always seem to avoid addressing the crucial distributional question of who gains and who loses and why.

The problem with these approaches is that they do not capture what most people think the welfare state does. It is first and foremost a mutual insurance scheme to which we all contribute when times are good and from which we all expect to draw when times are not so good. It works in this way because we are all at risk to some extent from the vagaries of ill health, unemployment and old age. The welfare state also functions as a device to transfer resources to people whose misfortunes we are unlikely to share but to whom we feel an obligation. Ultimately both of these functions — the mutual insurance function and something much more like traditional charity

— rest on some sense of shared values. A mutual insurance scheme would not work if we felt that some people were deliberately running their lives in such a way as to put as little into the pot as possible and take out as much. As for the charitable function that too rests on a belief that the people we want to help are the victims of misfortunes we can sympathise with rather than simply having made different choices than us about how to live their lives.

The welfare state may help a modern economy to function efficiently but ultimately we can only justify taking approximately a quarter of our entire national output through coercive taxation by some moral appeal resting on our obligations to fellow members of our community. The classic view set out so eloquently by William Beveridge assumes that all citizens of this country are automatically members of this community. We have duties to our fellow citizens in Bristol and Birmingham that we do not have to people in Bologna or Bremen. (There are fewer more intensely nationalist institutions than the modern welfare state.) We would all like to think it was as simple as that. But the argument which is beginning to surface is what if anything does this shared citizenship entail: is any behaviour to be expected? Can any conditions be set other than simply being a citizen of this country?

We can already see evidence of this sort of deeper question in the popular concern about foreigners claiming entitlement to British benefits, or benefits being paid to New Age Travellers. The sums of money involved may not be enormous, but the sense of affront to the community's values is intense. Most people belief that war widows should be receiving more in benefits than New Age Travellers — a crucial distinction which the technocrats preoccupied with measuring income and redistributing through means tests completely fail to grasp. Most people believe that someone sacked as a result of the recession desperately sending dozens of letters a week to possible employers is entitled to more help than someone not actively seeking work and engaged in petty crime to finance a drug habit. They expect these sorts of judgements to be reflected in the way in which the welfare state functions. If they are not and the welfare state becomes an entirely neutral device for transferring resources, regardless of behaviour then the willingness to accept the high levels of coercive taxation necessary to finance it will gradually be eroded.

This bring us to the great dilemma facing the British welfare state today. On the one hand it helps to sustain and possibly even encourages a greater diversity of lifestyles. On the other hand we feel less of an obligation to finance ways of living which are profoundly different from our own. You cannot have a big welfare state encompassing an increasingly diverse society.

The dilemma is vividly encapsulated in the two extreme models for welfare states in the West — America and Sweden. America is the most diverse of the modern, liberal democracies. It has the greatest variety of lifestyles and the most modest nation-wide welfare state. It would be difficult to persuade a Vermont farmer that he had obligation to help meet the housing costs of a Mexican immigrant in California through a federal system of redistributive taxation. Sweden is a small, homogenous, intensely conformist society and it has the biggest welfare state of any Western country. The dilemma which faces any politician, on the left or the right, is in which direction the British welfare state can and should be moving. What is naive is to imagine that somehow we can be as diverse as the United States, whilst at the same time operating a welfare state on the scale of modern Sweden. That seems to the be the delusion to which the liberal advocates of the welfare state have fallen a prey. It is the tension which lies behind much British confusion about the role of the welfare state. It is a challenge to those advocates of a welfare state which is neutral about behaviour, unconditional, undemanding. This will end up with a 'lowest common denominator' system much more limited than today's, which still rests on Beveridgean foundations.

We are being forced to confront a problem which some like to pretend does not exist; but which was well understood by the founders of the welfare state. Beveridge did indeed have a universalist vision in which every British citizen would participate in his scheme; but he in turn assumed that people's patterns of behaviour were and would remain intensely conservative. Where he saw a risk of what would now be called 'moral hazard', such as unemployed people who were not actively seeking work, he was happy to lay down really quite stringent conditions for receipt of benefit. Above all the national insurance system on which the health service and the social security system were to rest was intended to capture the reciprocity of the welfare state. It was intended to be a mutual insurance system into which we all paid when times were good and took out when times were bad.

Winston Churchill famously advocated national insurance when he served in Asquith's government on the grounds that 'I do not like mixing up moralities and mathematics'. He much preferred an automatic system of national insurance contributions than discretionary payments from local poor law authorities. But what that famous quotation fails to recognise is that the very existence of an explicit contributory system is in itself a type of moral arrangement. It is a social contract available to all the citizens of this country.

Sadly we have seen a steady erosion of the significance of contributory benefits. It was envisaged they would be fundamentally different from the means-tested assistance available to those who had not paid their contributions. Instead the combination of pressure from the Left to raise the entitlements of non-contributors, and from the Right to save money, particularly by cutting back on the earnings-related element in contributory benefits, has combined to remove any sense that serious conditions have to be met before one can receive benefits.

We need to be more rigorous, then, in setting the conditions which are a prerequisite for full participation in the welfare state. Perhaps the most extraordinary feature of the British welfare state is how undemanding it is compared with Continental Christian and Social Democracy. We could afford to be undemanding in the past because we just assumed that we were such a cohesive national unit that nothing needed to be explicit. We could all just assume that we shared the same values. That is changing.

If we look for example at social security benefit rates, it is clear that we do indeed spend a much higher proportion of GDP on benefits than many other advanced Western countries, though it is also true, as the critics protest, that our level of benefits is not particularly high. These two propositions are both true, and the point they reveal is that benefits go to far more people in Great Britain because the conditions for receipt of them are much more relaxed. This is the logic underlying Peter Lilley's agenda for reform of social security and its significance and coherence is not fully appreciated. The best way both of saving money in social security and linking the system more closely to our assumptions about behaviour is to ensure that proper conditions for the receipt of benefits are set and then enforced. Unemployed people need to be actively seeking jobs. Invalidity benefits should only go to the genuinely disabled. Help with housing costs should be conditional on those costs being reasonable.

At the moment one criterion for receiving Income Support is simply being a single parent. Many mothers now work when their children are at school and there is a case for asking that single parents claiming Income Support be actively seeking work when their children are of school age. Combined with Family Credit boosting their incomes in work and Child Support payments which stay with them as they get work, this would add up to a powerful agenda for getting single parents back in contact with the labour market.

We can learn from the continental welfare states how it is possible to set clear conditions for the receipt of some benefits. In France parents will lose their family allowance if their child plays truant from school. In Belgium you can lose benefits if both parents are not registered on the birth certificate. The use of the welfare state as a powerful instrument to reinforce some of the elementary rules of behaviour is to give it an explicitly civic function. If it is recognised that the welfare state is a powerful civic institution then we are entitled to try to use it to reinforce the shared values of the community. This same thought can also be put in much more market language: the welfare state rests on a series of contracts between us in our roles as receivers and as taxpayers and it is worthwhile making these contracts more explicit than in the past.

Unfortunately some of the rhetoric surrounding some specific Citizens Charters has tended to exacerbate this problem. The language of citizens' rights and of consumer power is attractive provided it does not exclude any sense that the users of public services have to behave responsibly. It is not right to call a GP in the middle of the night over a trivial matter; you cannot expect a place at a college of higher or further education unless you have got the right qualifications; the police cannot be expected to solve every dispute with the neighbours. Many people working in the public sector may like to think that their all problems can be resolved by more public money, but often the problem is that they are finding themselves less and less able to exercise authority and more and more under pressure from users of their services, who are impatient and demanding. The private provider has the right to refuse to serve the unreasonable customer — from the pub which wants its customer to wear a jacket through to the private school which expels the badly behaved child. If the public sector is to learn from the high standards of the private sector, as it must, then it is entitled also to set some conditions for receiving its services.

A second policy application which follows from this analysis is that we should also try to give greater local discretion for the provision of money and services through the welfare state. Whilst many people pay lip service to the ideas of great diversity and discretion, the widespread resistance to the social fund is a salutary warning of how in practice many people still want a uniform, over-regulated welfare state system. The social fund was a tiny attempt to bring a modest amount of local discretion into the social security system. It dispenses approximately £350 million out of the total budget now of over £80,000 million, yet it is still denounced as some fundamental attack on the British constitution because social security regulations no longer specify exactly when someone on Income Support is entitled to a payment for blankets for a cot or a set of gardening equipment.

We encountered similar difficulties with Access Funds for poorer students to be administered locally by universities and college. What is a sensible shift from rule-bound benefits to genuine local discretion was resented as somehow improper. Again whatever the platitudes we hear about diversity and local discretion we are still far from accepting it in practice. Anyone looking at this debate from the Continent would be amazed at this preoccupation with nation-wide regulation and uniformity. The local Mayor and Commune in France and the local authority in Italy have much greater power to dispense money in accordance with their judgements of need. That makes it much more possible to distinguish between deserving and undeserving cases in a way which a rule-bound system finds it very difficult to do. We could go further in bringing discretion into the allocation of benefits by perhaps inviting charities to manage social fund payments locally.

Two further policy conclusions follow from a belief in this sort of welfare state which emphasises reciprocal obligations and is concerned with creating greater local diversity and discretion. These negative conclusions stand against some of the current fads of the group identified as technocrats at the beginning of this chapter. One of the fallacies which the technocrats commit is to assume that the only thing which the welfare state needs to take account of is income and that our current social security system is a sad departure from the ideal of one over-arching means-tested benefit. But we may perfectly legitimately want to identify certain categories of people for whom we wish to pay more than others. We may want to say that a war widow should receive more than an unemployed single man. We may be willing to see students taken out of social security on the grounds that this is the wrong way of starting their adult careers — whereas the same argument does not apply for, say, pensioners. These are not judgements about the moral worth of individuals, but they are judgements about relevant differences between circumstances of different groups. There is a logic to focusing on categories of claimants rather than entirely on the incomes of individuals.

A further policy conclusion also stands out against the current trend towards maximising the efficiency of the distribution of benefits by trying to carry it out with the minimum of direct staff intervention. No cause is more popular nowadays than cutting civil service numbers, but we need to recognise that sometimes this will make it more difficult to pursue other policy objectives. One example is the early Rayner scrutiny which recommended that manpower in Unemployment Benefit offices could be saved by not requiring unemployed people to sign on so frequently. Now many unemployed people only have to sign on once a fortnight and for some it is even less often than that. Not only is this an open invitation to fraud it also risks disconnecting the unemployed person from the labour market if there is no reason for getting out of bed in the morning and taking the bus into town. The truly efficient policy would be one which had unemployed people signing on much more frequently.

The central message of this chapter is that the welfare state is about more than redistributing income and access to services. We also have to accept, whether we like it or not, that the welfare state must inevitably have an impact on people's behaviour and that we have to think about what those impacts might be. In many ways this is simply bringing us back to the old problem of moral hazard — that the greater the assistance offered to people in a certain set of circumstances, then the more people will be in those circumstances in future. It opens up the real debate on the welfare state between those are only concerned with the here and now, the visible and vivid circumstances of someone in trouble, and those who look forward to the effects of such assistance on people's behaviour in future. The dangerous short-termists are those who blithely set about expanding the welfare state without reflecting on its long-term implications for behaviour.

Chapter Seven: Reinventing Platoons

Fred Zimmerman's *High Noon* is one of the classic Westerns. Gary Cooper plays the sheriff who stays at his post knowing that three desperadoes, whom he had captured years before, were coming to get their revenge on him after their release from jail. He goes round the town trying to find anyone who will stand beside him, but no one is willing to serve as a marshal. The film was made in the 1950s and was taken as a critique of alienation and selfishness in America's suburbia. It is a striking contrast with a more recent film, *Witness*, in which Harrison Ford takes refuge with the Amish folk as he flees from corrupt policemen. One of the most moving scenes in that film is where they all come together to work for a day building a barn for a friend. At the end of the film the bell is tolled to signify danger and they all rush across the hills from their farms to assist the family and defeat the armed attackers. It is a vivid picture of mutual assistance in a particularly intense community. *High Noon* and *Witness* portray the two extremes of the spectrum of community engagement.

Many people in Britain, from all political persuasions, might like to see us edge a little bit towards *Witness* and a little bit further from the narrowness of vision of *High Noon*. The practical, political question is which policies are most likely to yield these values. It is the contention of this paper that a commitment to the free market, limited government and strong institutions, is by far the best suited for this purpose.

The practical test is what governments can do to strengthen the civil institutions of society. Perhaps the first thing that governments can do is not get in the way. The significance of the Government's deregulation initiative extends far beyond economic burdens on business. It should become a significant attempt to shift government out of what Douglas Hurd, in a different context, has called 'the nooks and crannies' of our national life. It is deeply depressing to visit the local Meals on Wheels service and to be told that they have had to cut back on the range of food for elderly people because of the Food Safety Act; to hear from the local children's playgroup how they have had to push up their prices beyond the reach of poorer mothers because of all the extra costs arising from the Children's Act; to hear from the charity trying to help poor people that none of its clients can now serve as trustees because of the financial risks which the Charities Act now imposes on them. The pernicious effect of heavy-handed regulation on local voluntary groups is greater than ever. Deregulation is therefore a crucial part of Civic Conservatism.

The Government must also resist the temptation to be a monopolist. It must allow self-help to stand alongside tax-financed activity. One area where this is particularly topical is law and order. The police have always been wary of Neighbourhood Watch schemes developing into alternatives to them; but the reality is that the police are so hard-pressed now that we can expect Neighbourhood Watch schemes to take on some of the traditional functions of the bobby on the beat. It makes sense for 500 members of local schemes to club together and put in £20 a year each so they can employ someone to walk the streets of their neighbourhood at night keeping an eye on their houses and reporting anything suspicious to the police. That is no different from the occupants of a mansion block employing a security guard to stand at the entrance.

The public sector now includes so many important institutions that enhancing their power is an important part of Civic Conservatism. A variety of devices for achieving this have been developed over the past few years. We are all now learning to distinguish between purchasers and providers, linked in new contractual arrangements through competitive tendering, market testing and internal markets. At the same time a new status has been gained by, for example grant-maintained schools and self-governing hospitals. The market — contracts, choice, competition — is being introduced within the public sector so as to achieve the authentically Tory objective of strengthening local institutions. Institutions which have been cowed by the centralising logic of a planner gain a new independence, holding one side of a contract.

There are two different objections to this line of argument. First, the free market purists will say there is no such thing as a strong local public sector institution. They believe that if you want to get the good features of choice, competition and the market you have to shift to direct private payment for the goods and services now provided by the welfare state. Wherever it is sensible to move to full scale privatisation and private payment, we should do so. However the reality is that there are going to be services which remain publicly financed. This is not just a matter of political prudence, but also of political principle and economic efficiency. A minimal state is not necessarily the most efficient state. It is a counsel of despair then to give up and say there is nothing that can be done to bring any of the good features of markets into publicly financed services. There are real decisions to be made about how publicly financed health care is delivered, what degree of autonomy is enjoyed by our publicly financed schools, how much diversity is to be allowed between different local authorities. Indeed increasingly we can expect to see political arguments between the Right and the Left focusing not so much on the boundaries of the state, but also on the nature of the state — how it discharges those functions which most people accept fall irreducibly to the public sector. The challenge is for the Conservative party to show that it has a radical free market agenda which can be applied within the public sector and which serves the long-term Tory objective of strengthening the little platoons within society.

There is also a very different line of criticism opposed to radical reforms within the public sector. For a long time these objections came only from the most blinkered public sector unions and could easily be dismissed. Now there is a much more subtle and authentically Tory concern voiced by those critics, such as Dr John Gray, who fear that a restless market ideology has replaced a genuine Conservative regard for the traditional institutions of the public sector. They say that the health service, the education service, the armed forces rest on a series of subtle understandings which cannot be caught in the crude structure of a quasi-market contract. They argue that the government is undermining the ethos of professions such as medicine or teaching. Hospital consultants, tea ladies in a naval base, scientific researchers in a university or Inland Revenue typists all feel as if they are the victims of a remorseless attempt to force everything they do into the straightjacket of a contract. It all adds up to a significant challenge.

The first reply is simply that the changes going on in the public sector now are no more than the changes which the commercial world has been going through for the past ten years. The modern management consensus is that large organisations should stop trying to micro-manage from the centre. They should cut back on head office costs and give greater freedom to local managers to run their own show within a clear financial target. The changes in the public sector need not be seen as driven by political ideology but merely catching up with changes which other large organisations have already been going through. In the author's own constituency of Havant there is a large IBM factory which has been given over the last few years much greater freedom from head office control than it ever enjoyed in the past. It can sell its products to other manufacturers, use alternative brand names, generate its own revenues. The speed at which the IBM factory in Havant has been given commercial freedom is much greater than the comparable process for the local self-governing hospital trust or the grant-maintained school. The pressure for change in IBM was driven by the rapid deterioration of its commercial fortunes. In the public sector it is the constraints on public spending which should drive new thinking about better ways of delivering services. There is no more deadly threat to any serious reflection on how to improve the performance of the public sector than the simple minded belief that if only it were not for 'the cuts', which are only the normal constraints over public spending, then everything would be OK. In practice it is precisely the discipline of, for example, the freeze on running costs which will drive reforms which would otherwise not have been contemplated. Public sector pressure groups always asking for more money can learn from the scientist Rutherford who observed as his team was trying to split the atom: 'we have no more money, now we must think'!

Critics see these changes as vandalism, destroying long established British institutions. But this is just another example of the British disease described in Chapter Two — our extraordinary capacity to become nostalgic about really quite recent institutions. The precious institutions they are trying to protect are sprawling empires only built up during the 1960s and 1970s. The sudden sentimental regard for them is on a par with the bizarre attempts at listing 1960s tower blocks. The NHS before reform was an elaborate monument to central planning, largely designed by management consultants, such as McKinseys, for Keith Joseph in the early 1970s. Teaching hospitals enjoyed freedoms very much like those now available for self-governing trusts until they were brought within the management structure of the NHS in 1974. Similarly grant-maintained schools enjoy rather less freedom than used to be enjoyed by direct grant grammar schools, which again were only absorbed within the system, or obliged to become private, in the mid 1970s. These highly centralised systems, based on an absolute belief in national uniformity, are very recent creations. They cannot be regarded as the historical deposits of generations of practical wisdom.

This in turn raises the crucial question of how we define the institution which we are trying to preserve. The institution which people can understand and care about because they use it and see it is not the NHS, but their local hospital or GP practice. It is not some great entity called the education service, it is their school or university. Those critics who argue that our public institutions are under threat are approaching the question too abstractly. It is the local institution which matters and that should be strengthened by the internal market agenda. The real problem is that this agenda has not been pushed far enough. Contractual relations should liberate the producer, but the trouble is that too often the contracts now being negotiated in the public sector are absurdly detailed. Instead of specifying what the outputs are, they specify in enormous detail exactly how the job should be done. The explanation appears to be that each side of the contract feels trapped by the other. Purchasers are so insecure in their relationship with the providers of services that they feel the only way they can guarantee quality is to try to write down in enormous detail exactly how the job should be done. If the producers of services genuinely felt that they had a variety of purchasers and if the purchaser knew that he could always buy from somewhere else this would give greater reality and credibility to the contact, which in turn would mean that it did not need to be so over-precise.

The problem is that too many of these relationships are still seen as essentially managerial rather than market-based. The only managers which the health service or the education service needs are within individual hospitals, schools and universities. The crucial skill now needed on the purchasing side is good buying and that involves being rigorous about quality but not to try to manage the entities on the other side of the contract.

We need to give the maximum possible freedom to the providers contracting with the public purchasers. The private finance initiative offers local providers enormous scope to cut their dependence on Whitehall for the allocation of capital and instead develop their own projects, privately financed. It should become not the exception but the norm. It is essential for strengthening local institutions' powers in dealing with the Treasury that they look outwards for private capital rather than up to Whitehall.

It can contribute to a wider transformation of the public sector as it buys in more services rather than taking on the task of delivering them directly through publicly owned capital and public employees. For example the public sector should never buy another computer —

instead it should be purchasing computer services from outside organisations which take over the responsibility for owning and managing the equipment, updating and employing staff. That is how Ross Perot began in America and Britain needs its own Ross Perots. It is the opponents of this trend who are the blinkered ideologues who believe that the public sector is all about owning buildings and employing people, rather than about delivering services.

Where employees remain within the public sector they should be employed on flexible terms directly by local institutions rather than on some uniform nation-wide basis. They need to break free of the old public sector pay rules — a freedom which many providers have been slow to enjoy. This should in turn make it possible for them to pay more to experienced staff so you can build up a career in one institution without having to move away or become a supervisor — one of the perennial problems which has weakened our public sector. These changes tie in with the wider Civic Conservative agenda. One sociologist has distinguished between two groups of professionals in any local community — the spiralists, who were moving through on their way up to their next posting, and the burgesses, who were genuinely putting down local roots and building up real local knowledge. The management of the public sector has left us with too many spiralists and not enough burgesses: that weakens the local community. Stronger local institutions can help change this.

As well as being able to look out for private capital finance, local institutions should also be able to sell their services locally. This is not a matter of the Treasury suddenly slapping on charges for essential services that everyone uses, but instead a liberalisation so that people buy extras which are not currently available to them. There is a misconceived aversion within the public sector to providing any sort of service unless it is free and tax-financed. As one modest example, many schools have been slow to open up after hours, providing supervision or quiet time for their pupils, although it would be of great help to working mothers, because they do not like the idea of charging for it, even though this would boost the school's revenues and would of course pay something to their supervisors. Similarly, GPs should be free to sell extras to patients on their lists — a sports injury clinic on a Saturday for example — which are never going to be priority users of public money. We need a private finance initiative for current spending as well as for capital spending.

Before we get carried away with this agenda for local discretion and diversity we need to address some big constitutional and economic questions. We saw one example of these difficulties in the recent report from the Public Accounts Committee denouncing the changes which the Government has pushed through over the past few years. It was a poor report, partisan in spirit and muddled in argument — not what one would normally expect from the PAC. Nevertheless it struck a chord. We do need a new constitutional settlement for the public sector so that we are clearer about the powers and responsibilities of central government and the powers and responsibilities which really lie with local institutions.

For a start, people have to be able to make real choices and that means genuine variations in services. While we pay lip service to diversity, we are really very uncomfortable with the idea that any aspect of the public service should be different in Bristol, in Birmingham and in Bootle. We find ourselves trapped in an argument which holds that diversity must mean inequity, which has to be corrected by redistribution, which in turn means centralisation.

There is no problem with businessmen sitting on the boards of trusts or grant-maintained schools being free from the control of local education authorities, provided that patients and parents have a genuine choice between them. We then have to accept the consequences of those choices, even if they are not choices we ourselves would have made. When the case of the Hackney headmistress who had refused to allow her children to see *Romeo and Juliet* because of its 'blatant heterosexism', hit the headlines many of us instinctively thought that the headmistress must be doing a bad job. But it was refreshing to hear parents of children at her school saying that their children had been taught better and had caught up with their reading since new headmistress had arrived. If they backed her and believed in what she was doing there was no case for the local education authority or anyone else to intervene.

We also have to allow providers to make mistakes and not to require that ministers are held accountable for every one of them. The author remembers one conversation on this subject with a permanent secretary who said that there was an important paper to be written entitled 'the role of the PAC in the centralisation of British government'. The fact is that if we wish to encourage enterprise and initiative we cannot also expect the sort of traditional patterns of detailed accountability which we are used to in the public sector.

Instead managers of these institutions must be under a different set of pressures — pressures from users of their services who are free to go elsewhere, pressures from purchasers free to place their contracts elsewhere. We must not end up in a limbo where we have both lost more traditional forms of political accountability and at the same time failed to gain the more vivid types of quasi-market pressure.

Equally the Treasury needs to be willing to loosen its direct controls. The trouble is that old-fashioned Fabian centralisation is a good way of delivering public expenditure control in the short term, even though in the long term it builds up pressures for ever greater public spending and it certainly undermines the efficiency of individual institutions.

One of the imaginative items in the 1992 Conservative election manifesto was the so-called 'popular schools initiative', enabling schools which parents were choosing to expand rapidly. But this has fallen a victim to the pernicious Treasury doctrine of the surplus place, and now a popular school cannot spend any money expanding its capacity whilst there are still schools with surplus places in the area. This is to obstruct the genuine operation of the educational market. It would be a nonsense in the commercial sector for a firm that came up with a better mousetrap to be told that it could not sell any more on the market because there was a surplus of mousetraps being produced by a less successful manufacturer. The Treasury argument of course is that a lot of public money is tied up in these surplus places, but it is worth investigating this claim a bit more closely. There is obviously some capital tied up in under-used school rooms, but by and large this has now been written off and is of little value. The main cost is teaching staff who are not efficiently deployed, but this is an argument for a more efficient and more mobile teaching profession rather than penalising successful schools.

This is certainly a free market agenda, but equally it is a Tory agenda for giving back real power to local institutions. The ultimate value of these institutions is because of the knowledge which they accumulate that cannot be written down in contracts or captured by a central planner in Whitehall. They have tacit knowledge about how to do things and must be given the freedom to put that into practice.

Chapter Eight: Conclusion

In his fascinating paper *The Idea of 'Character' in Victorian Political Thought* Stephan Collini quotes one socialist commentator observing a century ago that 'today the key word ... in economics is "character" ..... [the reason] why individualist economists fear socialism is that they believe it will deteriorate character, and the reason why socialist economists seek socialism is their belief that under individualism character is deteriorating.' During most of this century the debate between free marketeers and socialists took a very different turn: it became an argument about which set of economic arrangements would best deliver growth and prosperity. That argument has now at last been comprehensively won by the free marketeers. But precisely at our moment of triumph we find that the argument is not over after all but is instead reverting to that form which it took in the Victorian period — the last time free market economics was as intellectually dominant.

We are just beginning to open up these sorts of questions: it is an uncomfortable and difficult business. The critics fall into two camps. First, there are those who can be called the 'clever despisers'. They are an odd mixture of *bien pensants*, some socialists and neo-liberals, who do not think there is a problem at all. But they are a declining group. Many feminists now are ambivalent about the permissiveness of the 1960s wondering if it did not do rather less for women than they had hoped and rather more to liberate predatory male sexuality. Neo-liberals are beginning to recognise that the idea of the economic agent makes little sense unless that agent is embodied in a culture with a set of values — a lesson which is being vividly demonstrated in the fraught attempt at free market reform in the old Soviet Union.

The second group of critics are the pessimists who fear that we are impaled on a dilemma in which the free market that brings us the prosperity we all seek also undermines what Tocqueville called the 'habits of the heart' which make life worthwhile. Dr John Gray, the most distinguished member of this group is fond of citing Wittgenstein's remark that 'trying to repair a broken tradition is like a man trying to mend a broken spider's web with his bare hands'. On this view things are getting worse and there is not much we can do about it.

This paper is a modest attempt to try to see if there is a path forward which avoids the twin perils of dismissing the problem or giving way to a deep melancholy about our fate. The author has tried to address these issues before and showed how the free market and the community are both deeply rooted in the Conservative tradition and are reconciled within it (see *Modern Conservatism*, Chapters Five to Seven).

The politics of 'community' has burgeoned since then and there is a danger that this seductive term will become meaningless through over-use. The crucial Tory insight is that a community has to be embodied in real institutions which are essential to sustain traditions, values, patterns of behaviour.

The weakening of our civic institutions as government has encroached on them since the War is responsible for much of our social discontents. The political debate then turns on the conditions in which a rich network of such institutions can flourish. The argument in this paper is that strong institutions thrive in a free market with limited government. It is this commitment to strong self-governing institutions in a free market economy which constitutes Civic Conservatism.

A concern with the strength of Britain's institutions — both national and local — is at the heart of the Tory tradition. Addressing that concern is essential to representing the values of the quiet majority of the British people.

PAPERS IN PRINT   Price

REPORTS

OCCASIONAL PAPERS

OTHER PAPERS